HOMELESS DREAMS

"Dream Portraits of Minnesota Celebrities To Aid the Homeless"

Project Director

Matt Blair

Photography by

Mike Blumberg

Edited by Dan Hauser

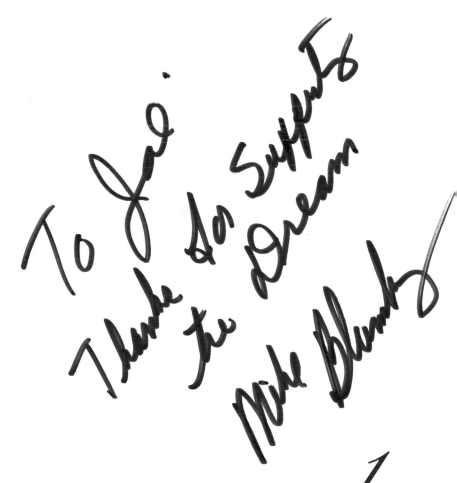

To Joe,
Thanks for supporting
the Dream
Mike Blumberg

Cover: Portrait of Bud Grant

"Homeless Dreams" is dedicated to the Homeless people in Minnesota and around the world.

Images made possible through the generosity of our sponsors Cub Foods, Golden Valley Microwave Foods Inc., and Agfa Copal.

Published by
Homeless Dreams
200 W. Highway 13, Suite 210
Burnsville, MN 55337

Library of Congress cataloging card numbers
91-092242 Soft Cover
91-092242 Hard Cover

Matt Blair and Mike Blumberg
Homeless Dreams
Includes Index
1. Celebriby men and women – portraits
2. Celebrity men and women interviews
3. Celebrity men and women quotes
4. Facts on the homeless

Book Designed By Rick Korab and Gayle Yarrington, Punch Design, Inc.

Interviews conducted by Kathy Crandall and Matt Blair

ISBN 0-9630190-0-7 Soft Cover
ISBN 0-9630190-1-5 Hard Cover

Distributed by: Matt Blair's Celebrity Promotions
200 West Highway 13, Suite 210
Burnsville, MN 55337

Printed in Minnesota

"Savor the warmth of fond memories, celebrate the special moments of today...Enjoy the quest of your dreams."
—Cynthia A. Adamson

To My Wife, Wanda,
My Dream Girl
With Love

Matt Blair

To my son, Mike. With love, Dad.
To Betty McDonald, my sister, who inspired my creativity at an early age.
To Gloria Gjevre, for her encouragement and unwavering support during the best and worst of times.

Mike Blumberg

Contents

5

Editor's Notes

Being homeless is no dream; it's a nightmare that affects more and more Minnesotans each year. It's easy to turn our backs on the homeless. But it's time to stop treating them simply as casualties of capitalism and start looking for creative solutions to the problem. That's why "Homeless Dreams" is such an important project.

Former Minnesota Viking Matt Blair and local photographer Mike Blumberg have set out to help solve the situation in their own way. They have gathered together some of the Twin Cities biggest names to act out their fantasies and jot down their thoughts about the plight of the homeless. The result is a humorous, enlightening book. While thumbing through the pages of black-and-white photography, maybe you'll think about the homeless and be compelled to do something to help and make some other people's dreams come true.

Although the subject is serious, many of these photographs are hilarious. Particular favorites include Eleanor Mondale imitating the Material Girl, Jesse "The Body" Ventura as, get this, a priest, KARE-TV's Paul Magers as Elvis Presley and KDWB Radio's Steve Cochran as a caveman. "Homeless Dreams" is definitely worth every cent, especially because the funds raised go to help the Twin Cities homeless. Blair and Blumberg should be applauded for their efforts. They have put together a wonderful product.

Dan Hauser
Skyway News

Preface

Homeless Dreams is a special fund-raising project designed to benefit Minnesota's homeless people. We have developed this book based on our mutual love of photography and dedication to the homeless.

Poverty is a powerful force that gnaws away at self-respect, suffocates motivation, and destroys hope.

There are countless working poor families whose combined hourly wages place them at below the federal poverty level. Victims of the slightest misfortune—a temporary layoff, a large medical bill, a divorce—suddenly find themselves in dire need of food, clothing and shelter.

In 1990, there were twice as many men, four times as many women and five times the number of children staying in Minnesota shelters as in 1984. Nationally, the estimated number of homeless ranges from 750,000 to 18 million.

The largest number of homeless are people who simply cannot afford monthly rent or mortgage payments. When these people can no longer afford traditional shelter, they must look to the community for survival.

In the past decade, 1,500-2,000 low-income units were eliminated in downtown Minneapolis through development and demolition. Only 500 units have been replaced. Incomes have not kept pace with housing costs. About half of all low-income families who do have housing pay more than 60 percent of their income for rent; the affordable figure is 30 percent.

Without a base level of material wealth, many homeless people lose their stake in their own community. Providing the homeless with hot meals, food shelves and shelters is critical to assure survival, but the real challenge today is to help people find direction in their lives, to provide the resources to enable these people to move on to some level of stability or self-sufficiency. Job services, transitional housing, and low-cost housing units are some of the ways to help homeless people beat back the crippling outcomes of poverty.

Catholic Charities, Exodus Division, is the recipient of the proceeds from the fund-raising efforts of the Homeless Dreams project.

Special thanks go to our sponsors, Cub Foods, Golden Valley Microwave Foods, Inc., and Agfa Copal. This project would not have been possible without them. And to the many other people who donated their time and talents to this project—thank you for your support.

Matt Blair
Amateur Photographer and
former All-Pro Minnesota Viking

Mike Blumberg
Professional Photographer

MATT BLAIR & MIKE BLUMBERG

HOMELESS Dreams

Portraits

PAUL DOUGLAS

Apollo 11

TOM RYTHER

The Old West

To או
Tom Ryther

13

GRACE LORENZI

Her Majesty Victoria

KIM JEFFRIES

The Torch Of Vegas

Kim Jeffries

"The Twin Cities have been a warm, supportive home for me professionally for the past 14 years. Anything I can do to repay that kindness from our community, I will do. Homeless Dreams is a chance for us to care for one another—that's the way it should be."

KIM JEFFRIES
Radio Personality
KS95-FM

BOB BERGLUND

Bon Appetit

"Cooking is a big hobby of mine. I was a cook in the army in the 70's and have dreamed of being a chef in a major restaurant. Unfortunately the homeless often dream of just getting a decent meal."

BOB BERGLUND
Former Radio Personality
WLOL-FM

19

MARK CURTIS

Sound Of The Streets

"I find it unfathomable that we as a society...can live, and eat and function normally in our day to day lives knowing that the homeless are out there... every night...in every city in America. We hear promises from politicians both on a national level and on a local level...and yet the problem still exists. Why? How can we as a caring, compassionate society allow this to continue? We can't...the plight of the homeless as we head further into the 90's must come to the forefront as one of the issues of primary importance."

MARK CURTIS
Former News Anchor
KSTP-TV

21

PAT MILES

Pat In A Flash

"All of the projects I get involved in are near and dear to my heart. The homeless project is perhaps one of the most important. All of us need to do what we can to encourage others to participate as well. We must all do what we can to solve the problem of the homeless. (I am a little frightened of going fast but I decided to be a race car driver because part of a fantasy is being a little afraid of doing it.)"

PAT MILES
News Anchor, KARE-TV

23

JOHN HINES

Highwayman

"After having lived comfortably, I cannot imagine what it would be like to live without the things that I am used to; people should have a place to go home to. I used to dabble in motorcycles, having owned six different bikes. My favorite was the Harley Davidson Chopped Sportster. I started riding at age 17 and rode for many years; I miss it."

JOHN HINES
Radio Personality
K102 The FM Country

25

BUD GRANT

Bud Grant

A Nation Remembered

"Now that I am retired from coaching, I have the opportunity to spend more time doing what I like to do outdoors, such as hunting, fishing, camping, etc.

"As a boy growing up, I would have liked to have lived with the Indians and experienced their way of life. It always bothered me that in the movies they were always the bad guys and always lost the fights they were in. I wanted to help them win. I feel that way now about the homeless."

BUD GRANT
Former Head Coach
Minnesota Vikings

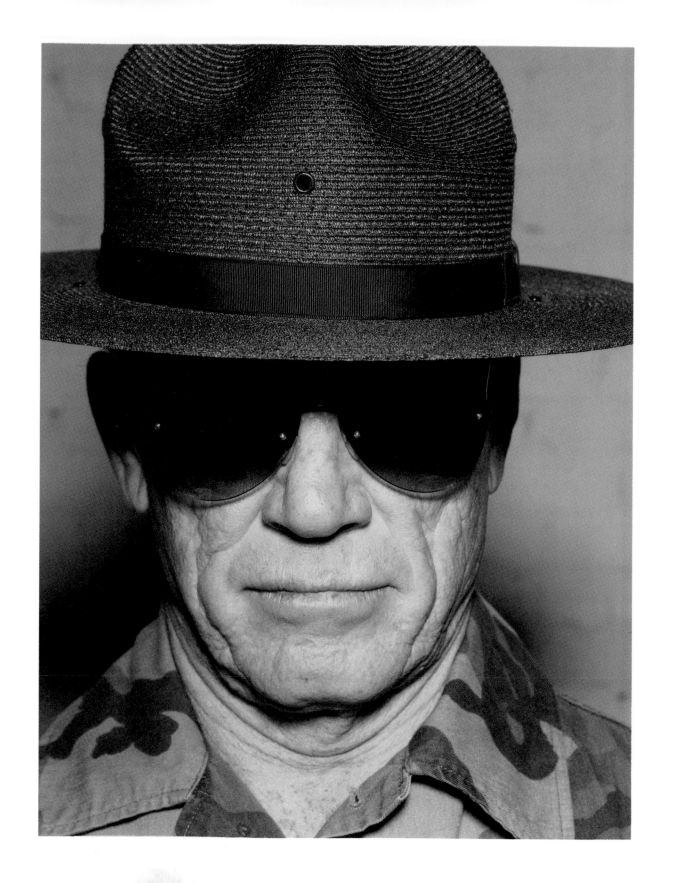

FLOYD PETERS

Improvise.
Adapt.
Overcome.

"Any person who has achieved success or improved himself has had help with the low spots in his life. We've all been there. The homeless are people who are at a low spot and somebody didn't come to help. It is time to turn our focus to helping these people."

FLOYD PETERS
Assistant Coach,
Tampa Bay Buccaneers
Former Coach,
Minnesota Vikings

STEVE JORDAN

Steve Jordan #83

Quick Change

"Superman seems to be a personality I can identify with because of my hectic schedule. Sometimes I feel I am so busy I must be Superman.

"But even in light of a busy schedule, I make time for worthwhile projects such as Homeless Dreams. In my opinion, awareness and understanding are key elements to the amelioration of this societal problem."

STEVE JORDAN
Minnesota Viking

SCOTT STUDWELL

All American Father

To,
lots of love
[signature]

> "It is so important to do whatever we can to help the homeless. My major concern is to keep this problem from escalating everyday and get it under control before it really gets out of hand. Two parent and single-parent families are being affected, and this proves to me that it could easily happen to any family. My family is lucky, so I am obligated to help other families."

SCOTT STUDWELL
Former Minnesota Vikings

SHADOE STEVENS

Intimidation

> "How can it be, that in 'The Land of the Free, and The Home of the Brave,' families could be without homes, that there are children with no roofs over their heads, and so many people abandoned on the streets with no hope? How could this happen in America? Please help."
>
> SHADOE STEVENS
> Radio and TV Personality

35

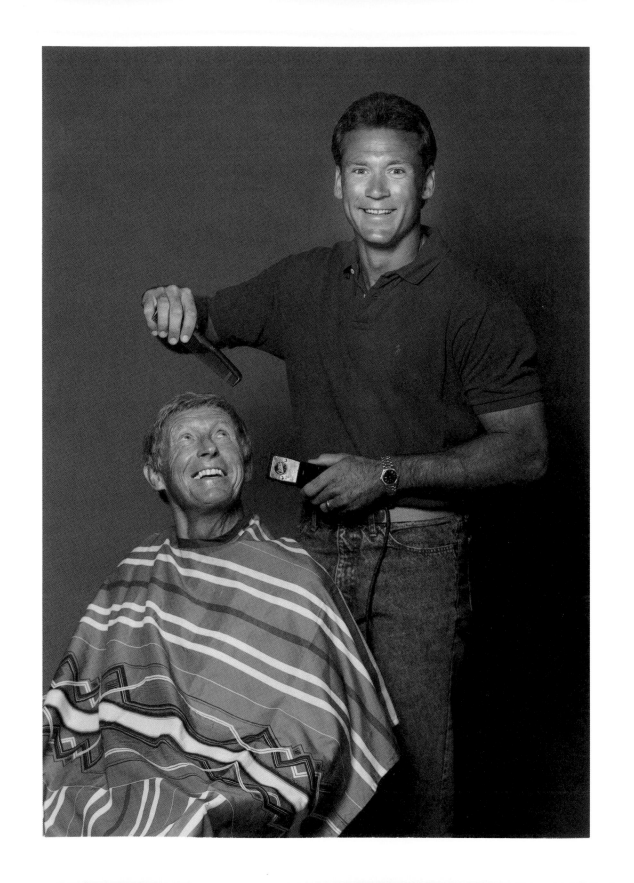

JERRY BURNS
WADE WILSON

The Haircut

"Homelessness has been a special concern to the Minnesota Viking organization. We are always happy to participate in any efforts directed at helping these people and increasing awareness about such an important issue."

JERRY BURNS
Head Coach
Minnesota Vikings

"Homelessness is becoming a more serious problem across the country. Everyone needs to do what they can to help."

WADE WILSON
Minnesota Vikings

JESSE "THE BODY" VENTURA

"I feel that it is important to give back to the community what it has given to me. I really believe that what goes around, comes around and that who you see on the way up, you'll see on the way down. Not everyone has things to give back, I do. It's just time to help."

JESSE "THE BODY" VENTURA
Mayor of Brooklyn Park,
Actor and Broadcaster

The Church To Window

To To

Jesse Ventura

39

JOAN GROWE

Take only memories.
Leave only footprints.

"Living downtown I see the homeless everyday and I am appalled at the lack of resources for them. I am eager to get involved to make their fight less difficult. I have always wanted to be a mountain climber and experience the thrill of reaching he top."

JOAN GROWE
Secretary of State

41

JIMMY "JAM" HARRIS

Jam Flight

> "Homelessness is like a rapidly spreading disease. However, unlike other diseases, homelessness can be prevented. We can all act as doctors by treating this disease by donating our time and talents to this worthwhile cause."
>
> JIMMY "JAM" HARRIS
> Flyte Tyme Productions

43

GEORGE LATIMER

A Soap Opera

"For a cause as important as this, I am prepared to take the risk of looking foolish. I am deeply committed to the homeless because they are people who, often through no fault of their own, have been left out in the cold. It could happen to your or to me. However unlike you and me, they have no home, shelter or security that we take for granted."

GEORGE LATIMER
Former Mayor of St. Paul
Dean of Hamline
University School of Law

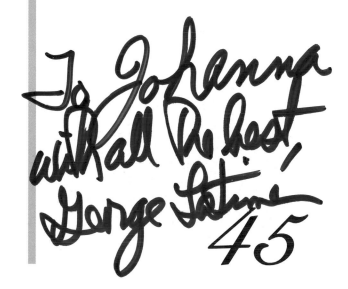

To Johanna
with all the best,
George Latimer
45

GRETCHEN CARLSON

Decisions

"When I was Miss America, I didn't get to spend as much time as I would have liked in Minnesota doing things for the community. Homelessness is a problem that affects everyone...not just the unfortunate who've fallen between the cracks of society. It's a problem that's not just going to go away on its own. There's an attitude in our country that no one individually can make a difference. I believe in individuals achieving goals...but I also believe you only get there by helping others along the way. I hope little girls know they can be anything they want to be...Miss America or a Supreme Court Justice."

GRETCHEN CARLSON
Former Miss America

ASHA BLAKE

Ahoy Mate

"I decided to become involved with the Homeless Dreams project because I believe we all need to help one another.

"I think we are all brothers and sisters in life and it's time we start acting that way."

ASHA BLAKE
Reporter, KARE-TV

PAUL MAGERS

Flashback

"This is a great way for me to have the opportunity to help the homeless. It is unique and unusual, but most importantly, fun. This is the first project I have dedicated my time to that is for the homeless, and it is an excellent way to help people."

PAUL MAGERS
News Anchor, KARE-TV

ANN BANCROFT

Polar Express

"For someone who travels around about half a year in a tent, I feel like I have a little appreciation of what it's like to be cold. It certainly makes a difference to me as I'm driving around in the Minneapolis/ St. Paul area and see folks out on the street and know that they don't have *any* sort of shelter. This is an easy cause to help out with."

ANN BANCROFT
Explorer

DAVE DAHL

Windchill

To Jo Bru!

Dave Dahl

"Enduring the type of severe weathers that the Eskimos face is something the homeless do every day, especially during Minnesota's cold winters. Anything we can do to help is taking a step in the right direction. We need to create an awareness of this problem so we can help find homes for everyone."

DAVE DAHL,
Meteorologist, KSTP-TV

THE OAK RIDGE BOYS

Minnesota Quad Sports

"We make a strong effort to do things together as a group when it comes to helping charity; it's a special honor to help Matt Blair's charities. Being Minnesota sports figures worked out well because there are four of us and four good teams in Minnesota."

STEVE SANDERS

"Dressing as a hockey player was only natural because I have owned hockey teams in the past. I also happen to be a fan of the Minnesota North Stars. I think it's great when entertainment and athletics can work together to help those in need—namely the homeless."

RICHARD STERBAN

"Most importantly this is such a great project that has the ability to help so many homeless people. It's also fun! I love basketball and it felt great to be a part of something so worthwhile."

DUANE ALLEN

"It feels great to be doing something to help the plight of the homeless. It has become a terrible problem in our country and these people really need our help. We love Minnesota and are big Minnesota sports fans and we are happy to have the chance to give something back to this wonderful state."

JOE BONSALL

The Oak Ridge Boys

57

PATTY WETTERLING

A Mother's Hope

Keep your hopes high!
Patty Wetterling

'This project is very significant to my family and me because we have a dream, a dream we need to keep alive in the hearts of a lot of people. Homeless Dreams symbolically describes Jacob. He is not home yet, he is homeless. Until he returns we will fight to keep our dream alive and to bring Jacob home where he belongs. We dream of a better world for our children."

PATTY WETTERLING
Mother of Jacob Wetterling

59

MICHAEL J. DOUGLAS "DONUTS"

Your Worst Nightmare

"The homeless people do not start out as nameless, faceless people living on the streets. I was even homeless for six months. I was unemployed and on food stamps, but because I was given the chance to rise above poverty, I earned my dignity. The homeless started in a place of position as we all do and they need to be given a chance to succeed. Our job is to give them an opportunity to bring themselves back to a place of dignity."

MICHAEL J. DOUGLAS
"DONUTS"
Radio Personality, KS95-FM

61

CHUCK KNAPP

"Abraham Lincoln was a President who helped the poor and downtrodden. His vision showed us that a segregated society would tear itself apart. He raised the social consciousness of people in America. It's too bad all the women weren't freed at the same time."

CHUCK KNAPP
Radio Personality
KS95-FM
"Knapper"

Equality

CLEM HASKINS

My Old Kentucky Home

"It certainly has been my pleasure to participate in the Homeless Dreams project, which I consider to be a very worthwhile project.

"I will continue to do anything I can to help out in this capacity because I see it as a truly valuable venture."

CLEM HASKINS
Head Coach
Men's Basketball
University of Minnesota

BARBARA CARLSON

Rome Wasn't Built In A Day

ROCCO ALTOBELLI

Rocco

"As a young teen in the late 50's, I had a summer job working with the railroad. This is where I first came in contact with Hobo's as they were called in those days. Now that 40 years have passed, the only thing that has changed is their name, now they're called homeless.

"I am very excited to be part of a movement that is doing something about this American tragedy, along with being able to do something that will change the plight of the homeless."

ROCCO ALTOBELLI
Owner
Altobella Hair Products, Inc.

ELEANOR MONDALE

Jo!
Thanks for your help
Eleanor Mondale

Vogue

"I have always had a true fear of being a bag lady at some point in my life. Our country is in a very desperate state of affairs, with the environment and homelessness being of prime concern. Handing people money is not enough: we need to teach those in less fortunate situations, and give them tools to learn how to cope."

ELEANOR MONDALE
Former Radio Personality
WLOL

M.E. STEWART

Signatures Of Design

73

STEVE COCHRAN

Primitive Rock

> "There's no cause more important today than the homeless. It is my hope that homelessness is not a trendy issue; that we will be as interested in it two years from now as we are today."
>
> STEVE COCHRAN
> Radio Personality
> KDWB FM

JO
WAN
Mufi
IPSO
FACTO

WAIN McFARLANE

Heritage

"I have very great problems with the homeless situation in America as well as in Minneapolis locally. I've traveled more than most people have and I've been from San Francisco to New York to Germany to Tokyo and there are homeless everywhere. I have problems with large buildings being built and standing empty that could be kept warm in the winter—especially in the colds of Minnesota."

WAIN McFARLANE
Ipso Facto

C.J.

Lady In The Locker Room

"This is one of the richest countries in the world. I just don't think there is any reason that we should have homeless people."

C. J.
Columnist
Star Tribune

TONY BOUZA

Elementary

> "The sight of a homeless person should be a rebuke to any citizen.
>
> "It is our obligation to feed the hungry and shelter the homeless."
>
> TONY BOUZA
> Former Minneapolis
> Police Chief

81

SHIRLEY WITHERSPOON

Spotlight On Jazz

"To have people in this country who are homeless, is, to say the least, appalling. They seem so distant, but they are really so very close. As a matter of fact, many people are only one or two paychecks away from being homeless themselves…think about it."

SHIRLEY WITHERSPOON
Jazz Singer

HARVEY MACKAY

Mackay

DEAR JO,
DIVE IN!

Harvey Mackay

85

DR. JOHN S. NAJARIAN

Skyblade

The homeless situation tears at the heartstrings. I see it as an embarrassment to the U.S. considering that we are viewed as the richest country in the world.

"Each of us needs to do whatever we can to ensure a healthy and dignified life for everyone."

DR. JOHN S. NAJARIAN
Jay Phillips Chair in Surgery;
Chairman,
Department of Surgery
University of Minnesota

Hi Jo!
Whee!.
Barbara
Flanagan

BARBARA FLANAGAN

The Sixth Dolly

"Ever since I interviewed the original 'Dolly,' Carol Channing, and the other Dollys, Pearl Bailey, Ethyl Merman, Mary Martin and Ginger Rogers, I've wanted to be a Broadway star. The reason I wanted to get involved with Homeless Dreams is because it helped a fine cause and a great charity. In the forty years I've been covering events, this is the most creative, imaginative, original and out of the ordinary idea I've ever heard of. We all need a dream that could come true someday."

BARBARA FLANAGAN
Columnist
Star Tribune

MARK ROSEN

Cantina

"We as a public can do a much better job of making life a lot easier for homeless people. We all too often look at the homeless as people who got a bad break—it could happen to anyone. We should focus on it a lot more than on some of the other issues that our politicians feel are important. In fact, this Christmas, my wife and I are not exchanging gifts—we've decided that as a family we are going to do something for the homeless—seriously. It's an important issue in our house."

MARK ROSEN
Sports Anchor, WCCO·TV

91

TYRONE CORBIN

Me & The Chief

AL NEWMAN

The Postman And The Poodle

95

BOBBY SMITH

Point.
Set.
Match.

"The 'homelessness' is a problem with as many causes as there are homeless people.

"Education, compassion, decent jobs and hope must be at the root of the solution."

BOBBY SMITH
Minnesota North Stars

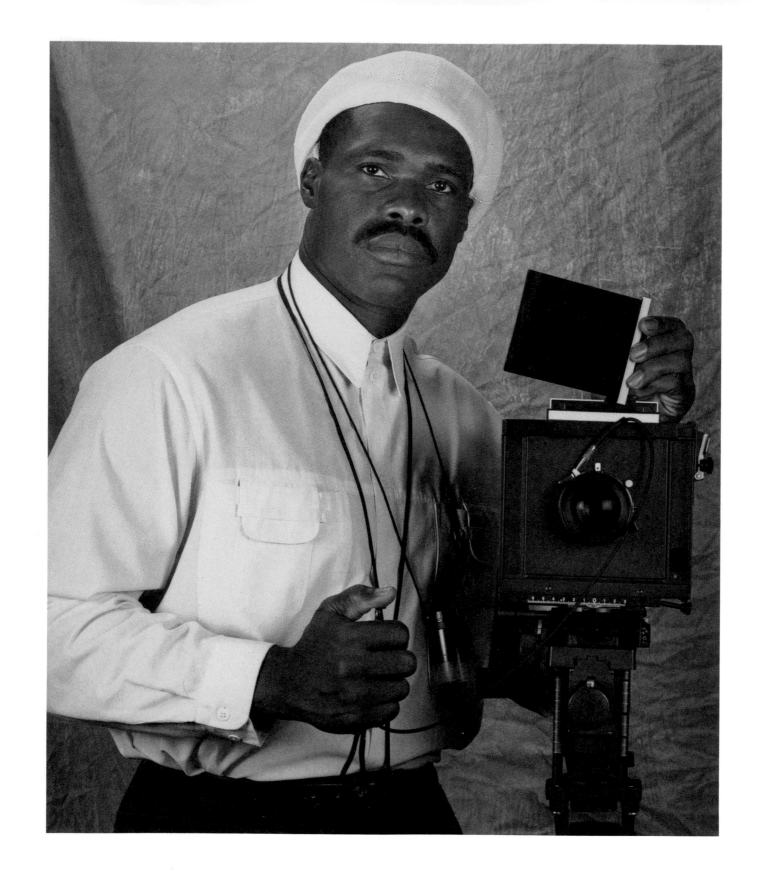

MATT BLAIR

F-Stop

"Minnesota is very cold in the winter. Homeless people have died. I feel homeless people have given up on themselves and their American Dreams. As a country we must reach out and help them get back their dignity. And never, never, never give up the American Dream.

MATT BLAIR
Former Minnesota Viking

This project owes its real life
to the early encouragement of
a dream...

Cub Foods
Gold Sponsor

Golden Valley Microwave, Inc.
Silver Sponsor

Agfa Copal
Bronze Sponsor

Acknowledgements

A sincere thank you to the many people who contributed in their many special ways to this project, especially:

Cynthia A. Adamson
Alaskan Fur Company, Inc.
Dick Ames Farm
Amesbarry Barbers
Stephanie Anderson
The Athlete's Foot
Bachman's
Sheri Bethke
Wanda Blair
Brum Light
Tim Buck
Catholic Charities Volunteers
Rick Russel, Catholic Charities
City of Mpls. Park and Recreation
Chip DeMann
Kathy Crandall Dornfeld
Eden Prairie Fire Department
Emerald Evenings
Ed Erickson

Debbie Estes
everGreeneJewelers
Felicia J. Boyd, Faegre & Benson
Gabriela's
Gloria Gjevre
Don Haller
Dan Hauser
Holly Henson
Dawn Hilbert
Kevin Hovey
Marguerite Ann Hulbert
Ben Jensen
David Jensen
Gene Jensen
Knights Formal Wear, Inc.
Kim LeSage
Long Hall Photo Lab
David Maderich
Lisa Matter

Joe McDonald
Midwest Delivery
Midwest Mountaineering
Minnesota State Patrol
NASA
Natl. Association of Letter Carriers
Dee Nelson
Nemer, Fieger & Associates, Inc.
   Advertising/Marketing/PR
Northwest Airlines
N.W. Moulding & Picture Frame Co.
Curt Overlander
Pearl Vision
John Pedersen
John Pellegrene
Pet Ranch
Pixel the dog
The Proper Setting
Rick Korab, Punch Design, Inc.

Cindy Rae
REI
Megan Ryan
Steve Rosso
Schmitt Music Company
Mike Schultz
Lou Anne Sexton
Sinar Bron Inc.
Kevin Snell
Theatrical Costume Company
Pam Thompson
Urban Communications
U.S. Army Reserve–Minnesota
West Photo
Craig Wetherbee
Jan Wheeler
Whitney Hotel
Matthew Witchell
Kenn Wolfe

To our families and friends, with whom we've spent far too little time during this project.
We are grateful for their help, patience, and understanding.

To the 45 celebrities who appear in this book and exhibitions.
Thank you for your love, your time, your gifts, and your dreams you have shared with all of us.

Matt Blair
Mike Blumberg

Index

Matt Blair

An All-Pro linebacker for the Minnesota Vikings from 1974 to 1985, Matt Blair enjoyed an exemplary sports career. Starring in two Super Bowls, he was selected as team captain for eight seasons (1979-1986), honored with six consecutive Pro Bowl appearances, voted NFLP Most Valuable Linebacker in 1980, and played in three NFC Division Championships. Throughout his career with the Vikings, Matt committed many personal hours to supporting a number of charitable programs, and learned photography using his teammates as subjects.

In 1987 Matt Blair formed an advertising, marketing and sports promotion company, Matt Blair's Celebrity Promotions. The company specializes in coordinating special events, including charitable and sports marketing events, and booking celebrities for appearances.

Matt is a graduate of Iowa State University.

Mike Blumberg

Mike Blumberg has been a photographer for nearly 20 years, providing images for advertising agencies, publications, and corporations. His firm Blumberg Advertising Photography, based in Minneapolis, Minnesota, specializes in people and fashion photography.

He contributes his photography talent to various charitable projects which benefit the homeless, and national and international hunger relief.

Mike is a graduate of UCLA.